EMERGENCY RESCUE VEHICLES

Michael Haenggi & John H. Holmgren

Motorbooks International
Publishers & Wholesalers

First published in 1997 by Motorbooks International Publishers & Wholesalers, 729 Prospect Avenue, PO Box 1, Osceola, WI 54020 USA

Chapters 1 and 2 by John H. Holmgren
Chapters 3 and 4 by Michael Haenggi

Motorbooks International books are also available at discounts in bulk quantity for industrial or sales-promotional use. For details write to Special Sales Manager at the Publisher's address

Library of Congress Cataloging-in-Publication Data

Haenggi, Michael.
    Emergency rescue vehicles/ Michael Haenggi & John H. Holmgren.
        p. cm. -- (Enthusiast color series)
    Includes index.
    ISBN 0-7603-0274-X (alk. paper)
    1. Emergency vehicles. 2. Trucks. 3. Helicopters. 4. Life-boats. I. Holmgren, John H., 1969- II. Title. III. Series.
TL235.8.H34 1997
629.225--dc21   97-8683

On the front cover: An Orange County Fire Rescue Division firefighter battles a Florida blaze from atop an ALS engine. ALS engines are fire engines capable of delivering Advanced Life Support to patients in addition to fighting fires. *Byron Rhodes/Code Red*

On the back over: High above San Francisco Bay, a US Coast Guard Sikorsky HH-60J Jayhawk takes advantage of some great flying weather. When necessary, Jayhawk pilots can use the helicopter's sophisticated navigation equipment and radar to fly safely in poor weather, day or night. *Nick Veronico*

On the frontispiece: A view of the side door of Heavy Rescue #56 operated by the Los Angeles City Fire Department. Built upon a 1995 Peterbuilt Model 377, Heavy Rescue #56 provides Los Angeles with the heavy lifting ability required to rescue people trapped in buildings destroyed by earthquakes. *David Bohrer*

On the title page: A patient and the crew of Rescue 44 of New Richmond EMS stand by on a Wisconsin farm as a Life Link III S-76 flares to land. Accidents in rural areas are frequently responded to by EMS helicopters based in nearby cities. In this case, the S-76 flew out from St. Paul, Minnesota, roughly 30 miles away. *Life Link III*

Edited by Lee Klancher
Designed by Katie Finney

Printed in Hong Kong through World Print, Ltd.

CONTENTS

ACKNOWLEDGMENTS

We are grateful to many people for their contributions to this book. For providing their help in various ways, we thank Grant Anderson, Peter Beck, Gary Bistram, David Bohrer, Lori Brown, Joseph Bueter, EMT-P; Lee Erickson, EMT-P; Greg Fuller, FF/EMT-IV; Jerry Gilbert, FF/EMT-P; Jeffrey Grosscup, George Hall, Nat Herold, FF/EMT-IV; Joe "Boom-Boom" Martinez, EMT-P; Red Novecki, Howard M. Paul, Greg Peterson, FF/EMT-P; Craig Schauffert, Brian Small, Barry Smith, Nick Veronico, and Mark Wagner.

We thank the following organizations for providing their support: 3M Corporation, Abberdeen Fire Department, AM General Corporation, the American Powerboat Racing Association, Lakes Region EMS, Life Link III, Los Angeles City Fire Department, Mount Horeb Fire Department, North Air Care, Orlando International Airport Fire Department, Oshkosh Truck Corporation, Roseville Fire Department, St. Paul-Ramsey Medical Center, and the U.S. Navy.

This book would have never happened without the dedicated efforts of the staff at Motorbooks International, including Lee Klancher, Jana Solberg, Katie Finney, Amy Huberty, Carol Weiss, Sharon Gorka, Carol Adamczyk, the Marketing Department, and all the rest of the employees. A special thanks to Tim Parker and Jack Savage.

Thanks to Captain Morgan for his well-mixed support, and finally, Michelle Dunnigan and Teri Jo Schank, RN/Squeeze; who each contributed in their own ways.

INTRODUCTION

There are an amazing variety of rescue vehicles in use throughout the world today. Rescue trucks, ambulances, helicopters and airplanes, and a variety of watercraft all operate in this role. To understand the scope of the vehicles covered in this book, a little background information about the field of emergency services is in order. This field has grown tremendously over the last three decades and has become more specialized and better defined in the process. In that time, the term rescue has come to refer to the removal of a victim from a dangerous or inescapable situation. Removal from a burning building would certainly fit this definition, as would removal from a mountain top, a mangled automobile, or a soda machine.

For the purposes of this book, we consider rescue vehicles to be those whose purpose is to intervene in some type of life-threatening situation by transporting personnel and equipment to the scene. While this encompasses all of the vehicles found herein, you will notice chapter one covers rescue trucks. In the field of emergency services, ground units used primarily to remove victims from dangerous situations by means of various tools are generally referred to as "rescues."

Chapter two covers ground vehicles specialized for patient transport—ambulances and the more specialized mobile intensive care units (MICUs). These vehicles are unmatched in their ability to care for and move injured people. While perhaps not as glamorous as some of the vehicles covered in other chapters, ambulances and MICUs carry out the bulk of the rescue work in the world.

Chapter three examines helicopters and airplanes now used every day for rescues throughout the world. The military's use of helicopters helped perfect the concept of rapidly transporting trauma patients from the scene and delivering them to a facility capable of surgical intervention. Air evacuation proved to be an extremely successful method of increasing the odds of survival for a critical trauma patient. It was then incorporated into the civilian sector—first through the HASTE Program in Minnesota and then, with much more success, in Colorado. Rescue aircraft have proved their worth for long distance, high-speed response.

Chapter four covers the vehicles used in water rescue. As the area covered by rescue crews has grown, the vehicles utilized to facilitate them have become more and more diverse. Modern rescue crews have incorporated personal watercraft, boats, and even hovercraft into their arsenals in an attempt to cover the variety of terrain in their service areas.

The variety of types of vehicles helps ensure the rapid response and care of the ill and injured throughout the world. These vehicles stand as a testament to human ingenuity and the great lengths we will go to come to the aid of others. One can only feel comfort knowing that these machines and their highly trained crews are responding to calls every day.

CHAPTER ONE

RESCUE TRUCKS

Turn on the news on any given night and you will almost always find something bad happened, and, more likely than not, a local rescue crew was involved in attempting to fix it. As mind-boggling as the jams people get themselves into are, the ways that others find to rescue them are even more remarkable. It's no wonder that rescue workers say, "Nobody ever called the fire department because they did something smart."

These daily catastrophes created the need for the modern rescue truck, a rig built to carry the rescue gear and crew to the scene. Valuable lessons have been learned from terrible and often tragic events, and manufacturers have used this knowledge to pack an incredible amount of gear and technology into today's rescue trucks. Rescue workers, in turn, have discovered how to use anything that their creativity and budgets will allow. As a result, communities around the country are utilizing the incredible services offered by modern rescue rigs.

Few emergency vehicles are more impressive than airport rescue trucks. Because airplane fires primarily involve flammable liquids under extremely hot and potentially explosive conditions, many operations are handled from inside the truck. This is facilitated by remote-control nozzles mounted in various locations. The roof-mounted nozzle releases a fire-retarding chemical contained in the red cylinder on the top left of the truck. *Oshkosh Truck Corporation*

Rescue trucks, unlike ambulances, are not normally used to transport patients. Their mission in life is to carry enough equipment to handle the emergency situations most likely to occur in their area. Rescue trucks can be called on to do anything from removing a child's hand from a bathroom toilet, extricating a trauma patient from a crumpled automobile, or retrieving a climber from a mountain cliff.

Many of these rescues can be done with minimal equipment, while others require highly trained personnel equipped with winches, booms, hydraulics, or other heavy gear. The latest rigs carry all of this and more, including ropes, powerful lighting systems, and portable power sources as well as medical equipment such as automatic defibrillators, oxygen, immobilization devices, and even IVs.

These high-tech trucks are housed in a variety of ways. Fire departments typically have a rescue truck equipped with the latest gear. Large metro areas are occasionally served by commercial fire departments that have the same type of up-to-date services. Smaller communities sometimes band together and finance a rescue squad often staffed with volunteers or request assistance from a larger service when the need arises.

The people who staff rescue vehicles are as impressive as the machinery they operate. Many res-

Squad 1 of the Mount Horeb Fire Department in Wisconsin is truly an impressive piece of apparatus. This unit is equipped with a 20,000-watt PTO-driven generator; a 4,500-psi, six-bottle cascade system for refilling firefighters' air bottles; two Hurst devices that power 10 available extrication tools from two separate reels; eight recessed telescopic 750-watt scene lights; and twin electrical cord and air hose reels. The unit can provide an endless list of scene support to the six-member department that it serves. *Red Novecki*

son is that the placement of these vehicles is usually flexible. A fire engine needs to be placed in a position that allows for the best use of its hoses, with the least amount being used. This decreases the amount of friction loss and provides the most efficient use of the pump and water available. Ladders need to be just about on top of the fire (as safety permits) to maximize the tower's reach. Rescue trucks, on the other hand, are usually free to work almost anywhere on the

scene. Frequently they provide both mounted and portable lighting and long, automatic cord reels for quick and easy placement of the lighting wherever needed. Most rescue rigs are equipped with at least one generator to power electrical equipment, and many will have two—a large permanently mounted one and a smaller portable one.

Many fire departments have several rescue teams, each specializing in one or two types of rescue situa-

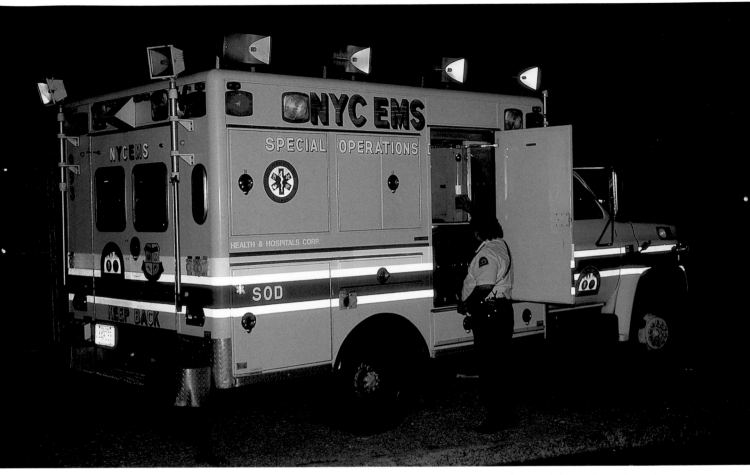

Big problems do not always happen with the benefit of daylight, and even when they do, they frequently last well into the night. Realizing this, New York City/Emergency Medical Services created a special operations unit to help light up a scene. This rescue truck can provide lighting and it functions as a command and communications vehicle. *Barry Smith*

tions. Others find it is more practical to train one group in many areas of rescue. This is a reasonable approach for a large, full-time service, considering that any given rescue situation can require multiple skills and techniques. For example, a water rescue will often require the use of rope-rescue skills, and confined-space rescue usually needs some type of extrication.

Most of the world's rescue teams are headquartered in smaller departments, however, and are oper-

ated by volunteers who donate their time to their community anytime, anywhere, and under any circumstance. While their motives and drive are comparable to those of workers in full-time positions, their budgets usually are not. So how do these small volunteer fire departments and rescue squads obtain these impressive, not to mention expensive, vehicles?

Large or specialized vehicles are often purchased with other communities, either through mutual funding

Getting equipment as close to a rescue scene as possible is critical. This Hummer was converted by AM General Corporation, a company that specializes in providing Hummers for just about any occasion. With their large payload, super traction, and long-legged ground clearance, these vehicles have proven themselves in the worst conditions. Not long after the Gulf War, they made a smooth and appropriate jump into emergency services where they reconfirmed their ability to overcome extreme terrain. *AM General Corporation*

Orlando International Airport's "Crash 80" foams down an aircraft fuselage on a Florida tarmac. This big Oshkosh is rigged up with a boom to elevate its master stream and give some reach to the piercing nozzle poking out past it. The elevated master gives greater distance to the stream and enhances the "blanketing effect" of the foam. This helps provide the oxygen deprivation needed to extinguish flammable liquids. The dark dome over the cab is a skylight to help keep track of the nozzle. *Oshkosh Truck Corporation*

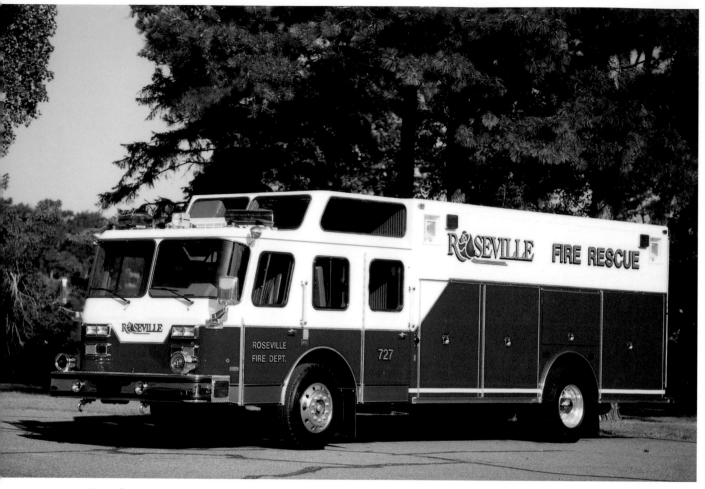

Roseville Fire's Rescue 727 is a versatile rig on almost any scene. Capable of seating up to 10 in a climate-controlled environment, it responds to all rescue scenes and all structure fires. An extra-large air-conditioning unit sits on the roof of the cab just behind the Opticom strobe (used for changing traffic lights). Placing the cab over the front wheels allows the large rig to be much more maneuverable on tight residential streets. *Red Novecki*

for one vehicle or by setting up a system of different rescue teams throughout an area. The latter seems to be a strong, functional alternative to each community establishing and maintaining its own teams. For example, several small-town fire departments might need more formal training and equipment in both high-level and water rescue, but none has the finances or personnel to have both. If they each focus on one area and

agree to provide the other communities with their service, all will benefit. It also allows smaller communities' teams to specialize and maintain skills in one area. Since they are freed from dedicating their entire existence to their "part-time, on-call, volunteer position," crews are more likely to remain with the team.

Another role frequently assumed by a rescue vehicle is that of an emergency medical service

✚ Heavy Heavy Rescue

The key to rescue is having the appropriate equipment and the ingenuity and creativity to use it. Heavy Rescue 251 of Aberdeen, Maryland, pretty much takes care of the equipment end of things. This remarkable rig serves Hartford County and its 100-member volunteer fire department. Used primarily for rescue situations, motor vehicle crashes, and large fire scenes, the 1993 truck makes about 100 responses a year. The Saulsbury Company built the rig for the four-station department—from its Spartan chassis all the way up to the sturdy boom that reaches just under 50 feet. Capable of handling a 14-ton load, the boom is useful in a variety of situations, including stabilizing rolled-over vehicles to provide safe access and patient care.

Barry Smith

Along with the obvious rescue capabilities of a crane, the boom is also used to lower a large aluminum box called the Trench Pod into tight spots. The Trench Pod contains various panels and timbers used to help make a trench or confined space safer by stabilizing the walls and other areas of possible collapse. Pneumatic devices are also carried for this purpose.

The immense rescue vehicle carries an arsenal of other rescue and medical equipment. Besides the standard rescue supplies such as a Hurst setup, ropes, and a variety of hand tools, 251 has many less-often-seen toys, such as a plasma cutter (an impressive device that uses oxygen and electricity to rapidly cut through metal). A cutting torch is also onboard. For rescues on lakes, an aluminum ice/water rescue sled is available, along with 100 feet of 5-inch hose that can be filled with air and placed around a large piece of woven netting, creating a raft large enough for several adults.

A variety of piston and high-lift jacks are onboard, along with an aluminum tripod used for lowering and raising people and equipment from manholes and similar places. Two portable light towers make night work easier and safer, and an air cascade system provides compressed air to fill firefighter breathing air bottles, greatly benefiting a fire scene.

As the department also operates the local paramedic service, the rescue is staffed with some combination of EMS providers. For this reason, medical and trauma equipment is carried, including oxygen, IVs, and immobilization devices. This makes the rig even more useful at a large rescue scene and as a first responder for a medic truck when needed. This is one functional and impressive piece of apparatus, and it serves its community well in a variety of roles.

The crew of New York City's Rescue 2 sizes up a high-rise job prior to the arrival of other responding companies. New York Fire Department rolls its rescues on all structure fires, using the crew as a primary interior attack team. All the tools for the job are carried on the rig (minus a pump and water). A door in the back of the big Mack allows entrance into the crew's second home. *Barry Smith*

(EMS) first responder. When rescue rigs can get to a medical scene more quickly than the ambulance, the rescue truck is dispatched to provide initial medical evaluation and treatment prior to the ambulance's arrival.

The rescue truck crew will then assist the ambulance crew when they arrive on the scene. Many full-time ambulance services staff their trucks with only two personnel. This is adequate for transporting the average patient, with one attendant driving and the other in the back providing patient care. With a critical patient, however, it is often necessary for one or more of the crew members from the rescue truck to

ride in the ambulance and assist with patient care during transport. Manpower can often be an issue on the scene, and a rescue crew is a welcome addition when trying to get a patient down from a fourth-floor apartment (you can rarely fit in the elevator), or when extricating a soapy 357-pound person from a bathtub (which occurs more frequently than one would think).

Large metal tools and brute strength are not the most significant contributions that a first-responding rescue can make to an EMS scene. It is proper training and a rapid "first response" to a patient which are critical in situations such as a cardiac arrest. Because

This awkward piece of apparatus is the Montrose Search and Rescue's answer to high-level rescue on vehicle-accessible cliffs. By lowering the front-mounted boom over the cliff, the team is instantly provided with winch-powered rescue hoist. *Barry Smith*

➕ Jaws of Life

After making sure a trauma patient can breathe, the most emphasized aspect of care is surgery. Because of this, "scene time" is the focus in trauma care. The longer it takes to get the patient to surgery, the less likely that patient will survive.

Clearly one of the most important events in the history of modern rescue was the invention of the Jaws of Life, made popular by the Hurst Company of Warminster, Pennsylvania. This gasoline-powered, hydraulic tool has several devices that attach to it, allowing the user to cut through metal posts, spread open doors and compartments, and use piston-type rams to help stabilize large objects or break loose connected parts, such as seat brackets from the floor. Because of this invention, rescue crews are able to extricate trauma patients from mangled vehicles in a fraction of the time it previously took.

The most frequently recognized attachment used with this device are the spreaders. With their two long, triangle-shaped extensions, the tips of the spreaders are wedged into a small space, usually between a frame and a door that cannot be opened. Hydraulic fluid, pumped from a separate device, flows through special hoses to the tool and spreads them apart to pop open the door. Unfortunately, this is not always as easy as it sounds. Many modern vehicles are made of plastic materials that do not provide enough resistance to the pressure of the spreaders and simply tear away without popping the door-latching mechanism. Also, thinner sheet metal and structural changes in reinforce-

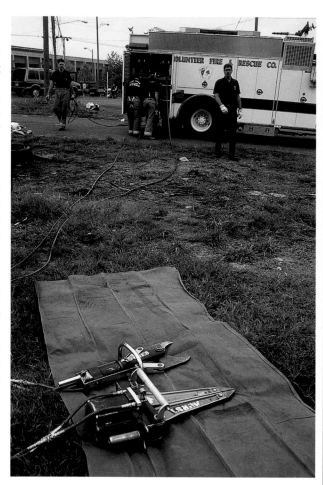

Barry Smith

ment make more challenges in finding the most stable areas of a car to "get a grip" on.

The cutters are an equally handy, if slightly less used, attachment. This tool looks somewhat like the spreaders but does the opposite job. Two thick, curved, scissors-like blades are used to cut through thick metal, most often the posts between the windshield and front door window (the A-pillar) or the front and backdoor windows (the B-pillar). Having done this, the roof of the car can be peeled back, allowing the patient(s) to be removed out the top. An offspring of these tools has been made available that incorporates both the spreaders and the cutters into one piece of equipment.

This relatively small, lightweight tool has made the difference in countless critical trauma situations. It's a great comfort to know that today's rescue crews can open your mangled car like a sardine can if your life depends on it.

Diversity is the key to rescue, and this setup can accommodate quite a variety of situations. The tall 4x4 chassis provides good ground clearance, and aggressive tires and a winch add security for the woods-roving rescue. All of this helps ensure access to backwoods lakes for water rescue and recovery. *Barry Smith*

The more roles a rescue vehicle can fill (such as EMS first responder), the easier it is for municipalities to allocate funds for these rigs. EMS is a popular service with the public, plus, a first-responder rescue squad will normally be on more medical scenes than fire and "rescue" combined.

The highest-profile rescue vehicles are decked out with large, powerful equipment ready to take on any harrowing circumstance. Dramatic, dangerous rescues that require these rigs are, however, the least common and typically the most straightforward. The true measure of a rescue vehicle and its crew is the ability to overcome the bizarre. Cre-

Though generally considered a firefighting apparatus, aerial trucks can provide a valuable service to a rescue situation. The most obvious and impressive is its ability to reach with its ladder to retrieve stranded victims. Additionally, ladders are usually equipped with at least a moderate amount of hand-held rescue tools and often are relied upon for auto extrication and other heavy rescue duties. *Barry Smith*

A recent study found various shades of light green and yellow to be among the most visible colors for emergency vehicles. Rescue trucks often find themselves parked in high traffic areas, so the more visible the better. This helps to explain the appearance of Johnson Creek's Squad 8. *Red Novecki*

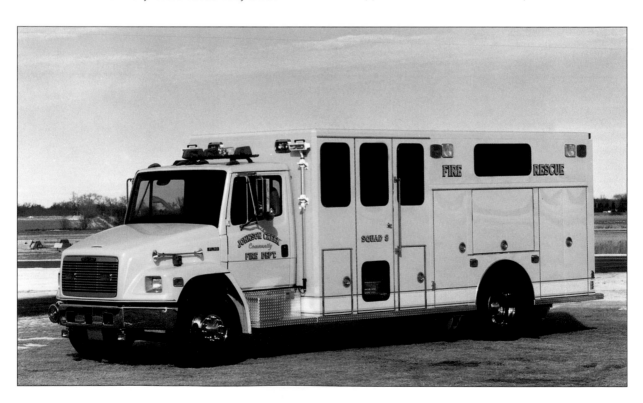

ativity is a necessity for rescue crews, and having the equipment and the ability to improvise can make all the difference. In these situations, smaller hand tools frequently are required because of their versatility. A person having a heart attack while trapped in an elevator is not going to benefit from a large truck equipped with a boom. Access is gained by equipment the rescue crew can carry into the building and the way it is used.

It is this kind of versatility that the modern rescue truck must be able to accommodate. Anything, anytime, anywhere is the standard. Fortunately for all of us, the industry has not remained stagnant and has produced the remarkable rigs in service today.

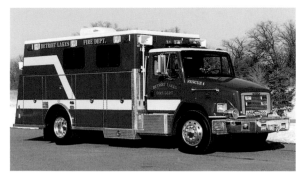

The trend in the industry is to mount warning devices on the grille and front bumber rather than on the top of the cab. This is in an effort to get them at eye level and audible devices away from the personnel in the rig. Note the siren speakers pointing at 45-degree angles to focus on intersection traffic. *Craig Schauffert*

Big Blue provides an impressive visual backdrop for a New York Fire Department (FDNY) demonstration for a group of school children. FDNY has a fleet of these bulky Mack rescue trucks and wouldn't trade them for anything. FDNY gets called more than 1,000 times per day and counts on these rescue trucks for everything from occasional EMS to frequent structure fires and rescue operations. At times these rigs and their crews are all that holds the city together. And now, with FDNY taking over the EMS responsibility in New York City, responses will more than likely increase. *Barry Smith*

Displaying two different but functional light rescue trucks is the Greater Manassas Volunteer Rescue Squad. Crash One is a utility rig used for vehicle crashes and extrication. It has a variety of Hurst equipment and preconnected hoses for faster and simpler use. Rescue 1-2, a Type III EMS unit, comes with its own variety of rescue gear, much of which is more patient-care related, such as antishock trousers and immobilization devices like backboards. *Barry Smith*

Because of their constant need to deal with the local terrain, law enforcement is relied upon for rescue support in many areas. When it comes to dealing with rough terrain, you can't do much better than a Hummer. This four-door sheriff's unit makes easy work of the mountainous landscape of Utah. *AM General Corporation*

A light rescue truck with heavy ability, Crash 1 sports plenty of powerful equipment, not the least of which is its Ramsey 9000 winch. Many modern rescue rigs are putting winches to good use at motor vehicle crash scenes. When vehicles meet at high speeds, they often attempt to become one. A winch goes a long way in separating them, allowing access to the victims inside. *Barry Smith*

There is plenty of headroom in Napoleon Fire's Rescue 806. Also featured are its convenient roll-up compartment doors, a significant amount of scene lighting (note collapsible light tower on roof), and an impressive graphic on the side. *Red Novecki*

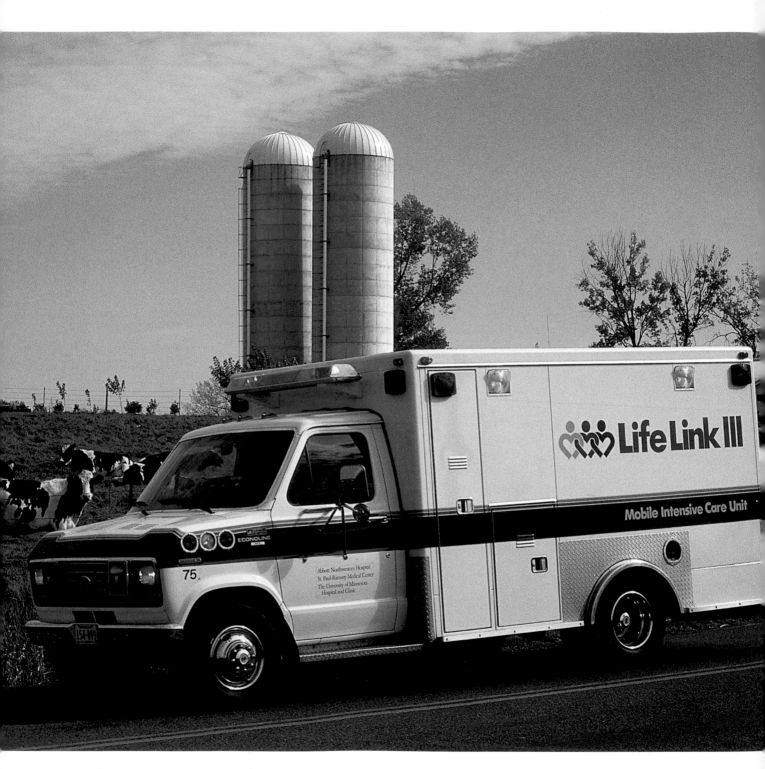

CHAPTER TWO

AMBULANCES

Ambulances have existed for a long time, serving as transport vehicles for injured patients. From hearses and the classic Cadillac station wagons with their single red flasher or rotating beacon to the strobe-lit modular monsters now in use throughout the country, an ambulance is designed to get the attention of the unsuspecting public.

Providing high-level medical care in the ambulance itself, on the other hand, is a relatively new element of public safety. Known as prehospital emergency medical services, this method of caring for patients has been quick to evolve and offers patients services wherever they need it. Nowhere is this more evident than in the modern vehicles used by EMS personnel.

Some of the modern equipment found on ambulances includes medical equipment like manual defibrillators, surgical and other advanced-level airways, IV fluids, and a wide variety of emergency drugs. They also carry electronic equipment such as two-way radios, cellular telephones, and inverters to power the vehicle's electrical outlets.

Many aspects go into the design of one of these remarkable vehicles, and as different services discover unique needs, new designs are created to facilitate them. For example, when members of the New Richmond Ambulance Service in Wisconsin felt a need to have serious rescue capabilities in combination with an EMS-transport vehicle, they took the idea to a custom manufacturer. Working together with the designers from Road Rescue Inc. of St. Paul, Minnesota, they created one of the largest, if not the largest, civilian ambulance around. Many of the ambulances built today are designed by the people who use them.

Ambulances come in three standard configurations, Type I, II, and III. In the early 1970s, the most popular upgrade from the hearse design was the standard or raised-roof Type II trucks. While considerably taller than the back-breaking low-rider station wagons, Type IIs did not offer much more in the way of elbow room or outside storage space. As EMS progressed, many services found the need for more space, so ambulances expanded outward and became modular trucks with the larger "box" on the back. These can be removed and remounted onto a new chassis. These vehicles come in two general classifi-

A Life Link III ground MICU en route code III to a small Wisconsin town for a critically ill patient. Life Link III provides critical care transportation to the Minnesota-Wisconsin-Iowa area via ground and rotor-wing MICU and nationally via fixed-wing. All vehicles are equipped in the same way and provide an extremely high level of care to the critical patients that they transport. *Life Link III*

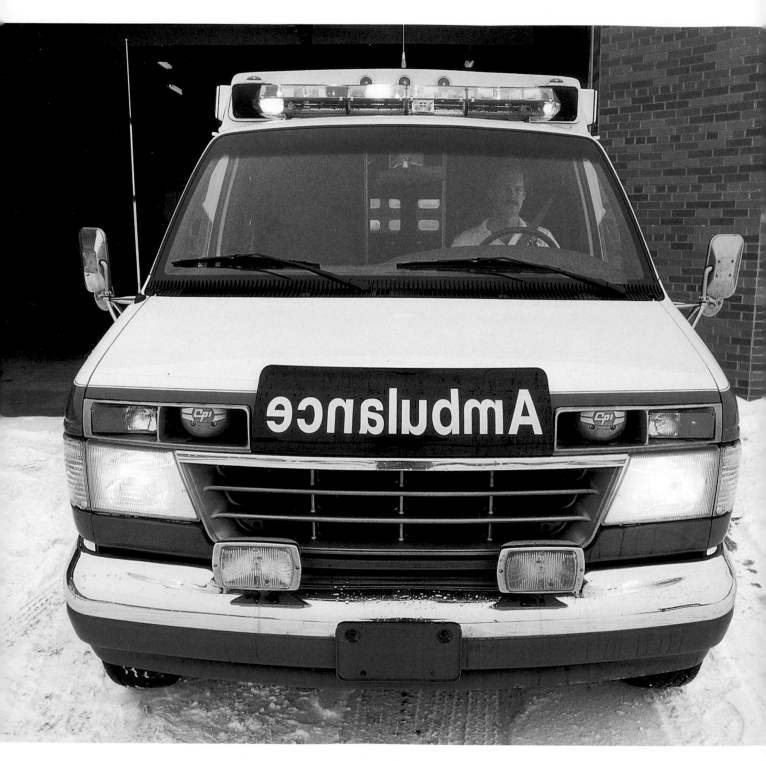

It's a long way from the bumper to the box on this extended-cab Braun. This truck also puts a lot of warning power in mirror range, including red flashers, clear strobes, siren speakers, and a written message made especially for rearview mirrors. *Grant Anderson*

cations: Type I rigs have a long-nose chassis, such as one that you would find on a pickup truck, while the Type IIIs have a van or "cab-over-engine" type front end. In all fairness to the slender vans, though, some large emergency systems such as that in St. Louis, Missouri, have stuck with the Type IIs and save lives in them every day.

In an attempt to bring some type of national standard to the design of ambulances, the federal government outlined a model in 1974 known as the "Federal Emergency Medical Care Vehicle Specifications KKK-A-1822," or KKK standard. It clearly describes visual and audible warning devices, modular dimensions, even paint scheme and proper headlight locations. For example, ambulances should be painted white with an orange stripe. Also, flashers (the flashing lights on the top corners of the rig or module) should be red, with one on each corner of the highest part of the unit. One clear light must be in the front center between the two forward-facing red flashers. All vehicles purchased with federal government money must comply with these standards. At the time the standards were created, millions of

Have a warning device! When St. Paul Fire got rid of its Federal Qs (large, chromed, mechanical sirens powered by an automobile starter motor) on the front of all of its medic units, the department had a bit of warning-device identity crisis, made obvious by this Road Rescue Type III. They soon settled on a slightly more conservative setup, unfortunately, without the impressive Qs. *Red Novecki*

Getting the Green Light

Grant Anderson

A significant advancement in emergency vehicle warning devices is the Opticom, a lighting system that enables emergency vehicles to change traffic lights as they approach intersections. The Opticom system uses a rapid-fire strobe mounted on the emergency vehicle. This light transmits both a visible and infrared coded signal that is detected by a receiver attached to the traffic light. When the signal is picked up, clear floodlights on top of the traffic light will turn on, flashing in all directions, except the side on which the emergency vehicle that tripped the system is approaching. In that direction, the clear floodlight will shine steadily signaling to that crew that their vehicle has control of the intersection. This allows all emergency vehicles approaching that intersection to know whether they have control of the intersection or not. If the driver approaches an intersection in an Opticom-equipped vehicle and gets a flashing light, the driver knows that there is another vehicle approaching the same intersection from a different direction and that vehicle will get the green light.

Shortly after the clear light indicates that the system has been activated, all directions of the intersection will change to yellow, and then red, except the direction that the activating vehicle is coming from, which turns green.

The signal receivers can be set to activate from between 200 feet and 2,500 feet. For traffic lights on highways where speeds are high, a longer distance is best. Shorter distances are more appropriate in a city.

An added benefit of this device is its strong optical power. This rapid-fire strobe is visible to the human eye and is one of the most attention-getting visual warning devices in the public safety arsenal.

As smooth as this sounds, real life does not always play out this well. The general public frequently assumes that if the traffic light has just turned green for them, it will remain that way for a reasonable amount of time. The flashing floodlight helps warn people the light is about to change. When an Opticom system changes the light back to yellow and then red shortly after the light turns green, it often goes unnoticed, and people sail right through. This problem was anticipated when the Opticom was designed, so the system records all pertinent information regarding the signaling event in case it is needed for legal claims. The system records the specific emergency vehicle that activated the system, the response of the system (if the light did actually turn green), and the times of all operations down to the second. This saves communities potential costs incurred from dubious legal claims, and it lowers insurance rates for the services using it. The Opticom has greatly improved the emergency vehicle's ability to respond rapidly and safely through thousands of intersections throughout the country, benefiting both the crews and the public.

federal dollars were being spent to develop EMS systems all over the country. The majority of services do not adhere to this 100 percent. Again, this standard only applies to ambulances purchased with federal money. Legally, an ambulance must conform to the laws of the state that it operates in. When a service covers more than one state, such as with some critical care services, they must comply with the rules of all the states they operate in.

911 Ambulances

As a rule, there are two types of ambulance calls: 911 and interfacility. The 911 call is what most people think of as an ambulance call. Situations such as a motor vehicle crash, a heart attack at the mall, or an emergency childbirth at home, are a few examples of the unlimited variety of situations that a 911 truck can find itself responding to. Thus, the modern ambulance has evolved into a diverse and functional vehicle.

The 911 ambulances can be separated into two categories, basic life support (BLS) and advanced life support (ALS). BLS units provide oxygen, bandaging and first-aid, basic airway equipment, and some oral medications, such as glucose gel for diabetics. They often are allowed to use more advanced equipment such as automatic external defibrillators (AED), advanced-level airway equipment, and IV therapy. BLS units are usually staffed with emergency medical technician-basics (EMT-Bs). ALS trucks use almost all of these things in addition to manual defibrillators, a variety of emergency drugs, surgical and other advanced-level airways, and a staff of at least one emergency medical technician-paramedic (EMT-P).

As the capabilities of the personnel and the variety of portable equipment expanded, so did the need for additional space and innovative vehicle design. The modern 911 rig will ordinarily carry some amount of rescue equipment, ranging from a pry bar to

A Type I ALS rig from the ski resort town of Crested Butte, Colorado, returns to its bay after responding to a call. Once inside, the ambulance will be restocked with supplies, have its batteries charged, and be thoroughly washed inside and out. *Howard M. Paul*

One of two identical units, this monster-medic from Missouri has an aggressive warning system, including plenty of blue lighting. Where legal, blue lighting has proven effective for emergency vehicles due to the small amount of actual light lost in the lens. Many systems have gone with similar ambulance chassis, using the additional compartment space for more rescue equipment. *Craig Schauffert*

hydraulic spreaders. The amount of rescue paraphernalia will usually depend on the type of support the service normally can expect from the local fire service.

MICUs and Interfacility Transports

Interfacility transports are from one primary care facility to another. For example, a 60-year-old man from a small town in rural Colorado is shot in the chest in a hunting accident and transported by friends to a nearby small-town hospital. Recognizing that the patient is too seriously injured to be effectively treated there, the hospital will contact a critical care service to transport the patient to the closest trauma center (provided there is a critical care service in the area).

Often a helicopter or airplane is used in this type of transport because time is critical in the

Every winter in Yellowstone National Park you can find resourceful park rangers transforming this Type I rig into "Old Faithful" by removing the traditional rubber and strapping on the tracks and skis. While it is restricted to the pre-existing trails, it's still the only game in town when an EMS ground response is needed in the park. As this is a government-owned ambulance, it was made to strict "KKK Standard" specifications. The downside? Come summer, it all has to get changed back. *Joseph Bueter*

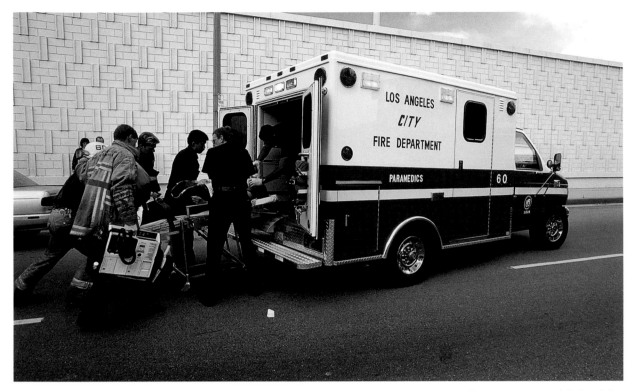

Los Angeles City Fire Department firefighters and paramedics work to revive a patient who suffered a heart attack behind the wheel—a typical call for a department that responds to nearly 250,000 calls for medical assistance each year, and logs over 1.75 million miles on an annual basis. *David Bohrer*

Rescue #104 is one of the 66 rescue ambulances operated by the Los Angeles City Fire Department (one of the largest departments in the nation). Strategically located throughout the city, these ambulances are LA's primary emergency medical response units. *David Bohrer*

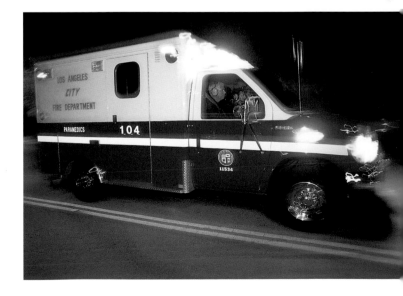

care of a trauma patient. For several reasons, however, many are done on the ground. Often the distance from the referring hospital to the receiving hospital is not great enough to require air transport. Or due to weather, air transportation, especially via rotor-wing (helicopter), is often too dangerous. Sometimes the expertise of a critical care team is enough. These ground mobile intensive care units (MICUs) are generally staffed and

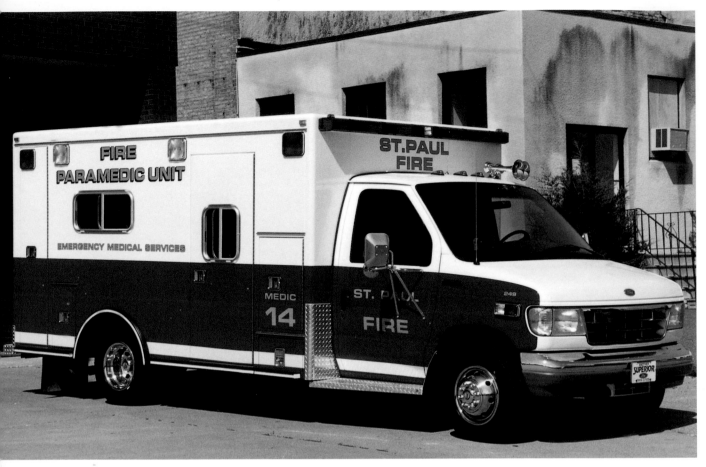

The St. Paul Fire Department eventually settled on this no-frills, yet very effective, design. Built around a Road Rescue "Supermedic," the classic "fire-medic" paint job is supplemented by a pair of high-mounted air horns. These can come in handy when you need to provide traffic with an audible tap on the shoulder. *Red Novecki*

equipped identically to their fixed- and rotor-wing counterparts.

The level of technology found on modern MICUs is truly amazing. In many cases, the equipment carried on one of these rigs is superior to that found in rural hospitals. Patients can upgrade their level of care the minute the MICU team arrives!

Life Link III, based in St. Paul, Minnesota, provides critical care transportation via ground, rotor-wing, and fixed-wing, locally, regionally, and nationally. Many of

the transports provided by Life Link III are in conjunction with one of the children's health-care facilities in the area. When a baby is born prematurely or falls ill shortly after birth in a hospital that is not equipped or staffed to deal with critical (or potentially critical) newborns, the baby must be moved. In this type of situation, the referring hospital (where the baby was born) will contact the hospital where the newborn will go and arrange for the move. A team is picked up from the receiving hospital. This team will normally consist of a

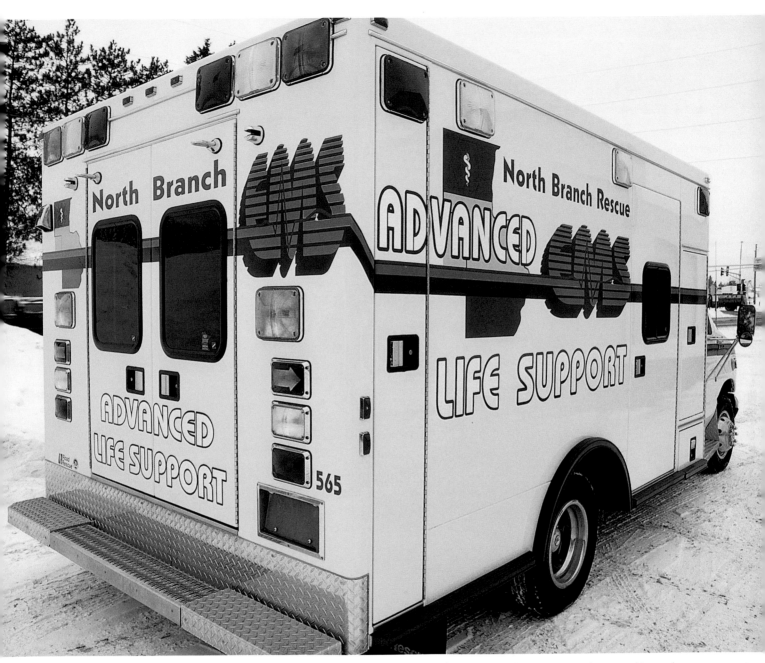

You're not likely to overlook an 11,000-pound, strobe-lit banana in the middle of the road. Add some eye-catching graphics and a variety of colored lighting, and you increase the visibility and thus the safety of everyone around. When the small community of North Branch, Minnesota, made the upgrade to ALS, it also upgraded to this design. *Grant Anderson*

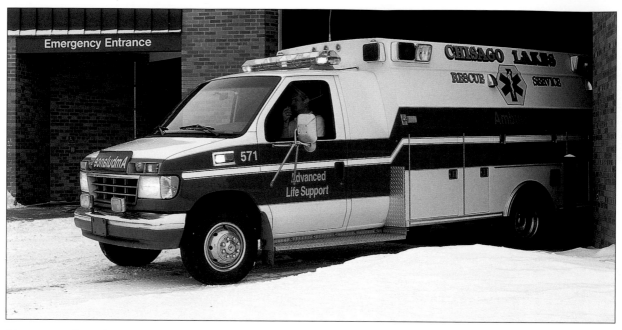

Many services keep their rigs on the move, providing coverage to different parts of their service area as well as neighboring ones. Often this means spending a lot of time (even an entire shift) away from base and in the truck. Because of this, Braun began filling orders for its extended-cab Type IIIs for many of the company's loyal buyers. These stretch cabs allow the crews to recline their seats back to "stand-by" position, making the ambulance a much more accommodating home away from home. *Grant Anderson*

registered nurse and a neonatal nurse practitioner (NNP)—both highly trained members of the neonatal intensive care unit (NICU) in the receiving hospital. This team will assume primary care of the baby while the ambulance crew assists them, both at the referring hospital and en route to the receiving hospital.

Out-of-hospital medical care has made amazing advances over the past 20 years, and the vehicles that make it all possible have evolved right along with it. From the local mortician's car to today's Type III ALS 911 trucks to the MICUs that can out-do many hospitals, the modern ambulance is an advance in technology that benefits everyone. The health and safety of everyone are supported by these vehicles, from the patient being treated in the back of the ambulance to the citizen who is able to avoid crashing into the fast-moving emergency vehicle because of its increased visibility.

The Little MICU That Could

At five o'clock on the evening of July 5, 1996, a Life Link III MICU was dispatched Code II (nonemergency) from its base to transport a stable newborn from a local hospital to Children's Health Care-Minneapolis (CHC-Mpls). When a neonate transport is needed, a team from the receiving hospital is picked up by the MICU to provide primary patient care. The responding MICU team (in this case, the Life Link III) provides support to the hospital team, such as with patient care, and more important, with equipment.

Upon arrival at CHC-Mpls, an eager neonatal intensive care unit (NICU) team greeted the Life Link III crew, which included paramedic Lee E. Erickson. The team consisted of a neonatal nurse practitioner and two neonatal intensive care RNs. They informed Erickson and his partner that the last

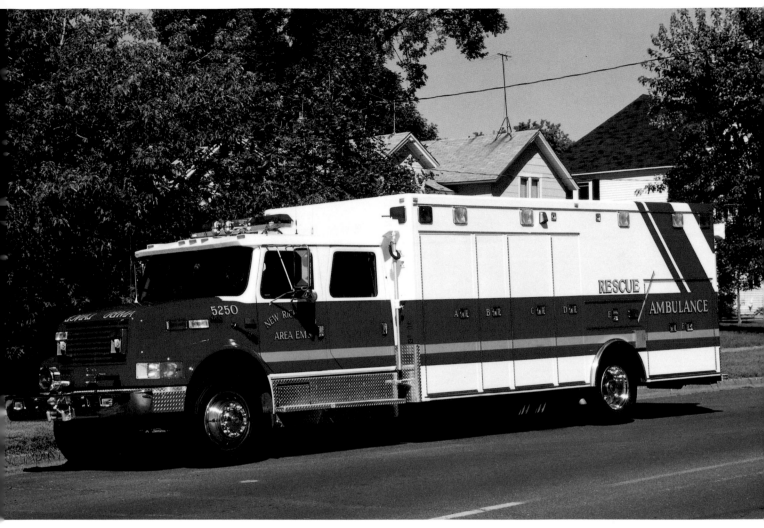

That's right, it's an ambulance! Without a doubt the largest civilian ambulance the authors have seen, this "stretch limo" of the EMS world is used for both EMS transport and rescue. While most EMS personnel would dread having to get this beast into a hospital ambulance garage, it's pretty tough to badmouth any ambulance with a shiny Federal Q on the bumper. *Red Novecki*

few minutes had produced a new emergency: premature twins born in the town of Waconia, Minnesota, approximately 40 miles away, needing immediate transportation. Unfortunately, there were no helicopters available. The routine transport originally planned for Life Link III would have to wait. "The call turned out to be much more than we had

expected, but I knew that we could handle it," Erickson recalled.

The Life Link crew headed to Waconia even though they were in a ground unit that was capable of transporting only one issolette (somewhat like an incubator, it is used to transport small babies unable to maintain their own body heat). The crew had

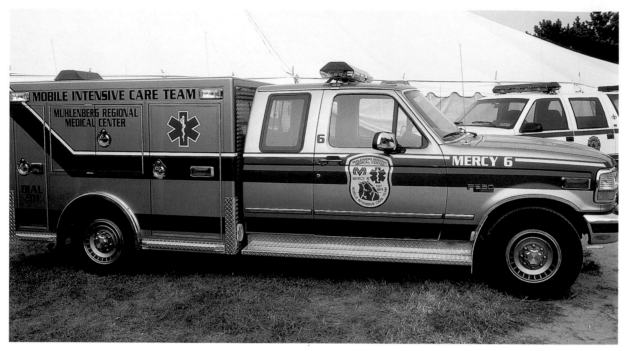

Out-of-hospital medical care has come a long way since this design was made popular by Squad 51 on the hit TV show *Emergency*. Many services use these utility-style vehicles as "chase cars" to supplement the local ambulance service with advanced life-support equipment and personnel. They are sometimes staffed with specialty hospital teams, such as pediatrics, to respond to a rural facility, stabilize the patient, and transport the patient with their equipment in the local services ambulance. *Barry Smith*

decided that because of the infants' small size, both infants could be placed in the one issolette.

The issolette belonged to CHC-Mpls and was equipped with one neonatal ventilator, used to assist the newborn with breathing. When the team reached the newborns at Ridgeview Medical Center in Waconia some 32 minutes later, both were in respiratory distress, requiring breathing tubes called endotracheal tubes, to allow them to be put onto mechanical ventilators. "Also, because the lungs of the newborns had not fully developed, a special drug called Surfactant was required to be given down the endotracheal tubes," Erickson explained. "Most infants produce this before being born, but these were several weeks premature and needed a little extra help."

There was only the one ventilator on the issolette, however.

"Fortunately all of our vehicles are equipped with a neonatal vent," Erickson said. "Both babies were placed in one issolette, [and] both [were] vented!" Had the babies been much larger, this probably would not have been possible. "Because we had the heads-up that we would need to run two vents in the truck, we had time to sort out all of our 'plumbing' to allow us to run both," stated Erickson. The ventilators

Many ambulances, medic crews, and firefighters from several departments participate in a mass casualty incident (MCI) drill. This drill involved a motor vehicle accident with a school bus full of children. With doors open, a Type II ambulance stands by to transport. *Howard M. Paul*

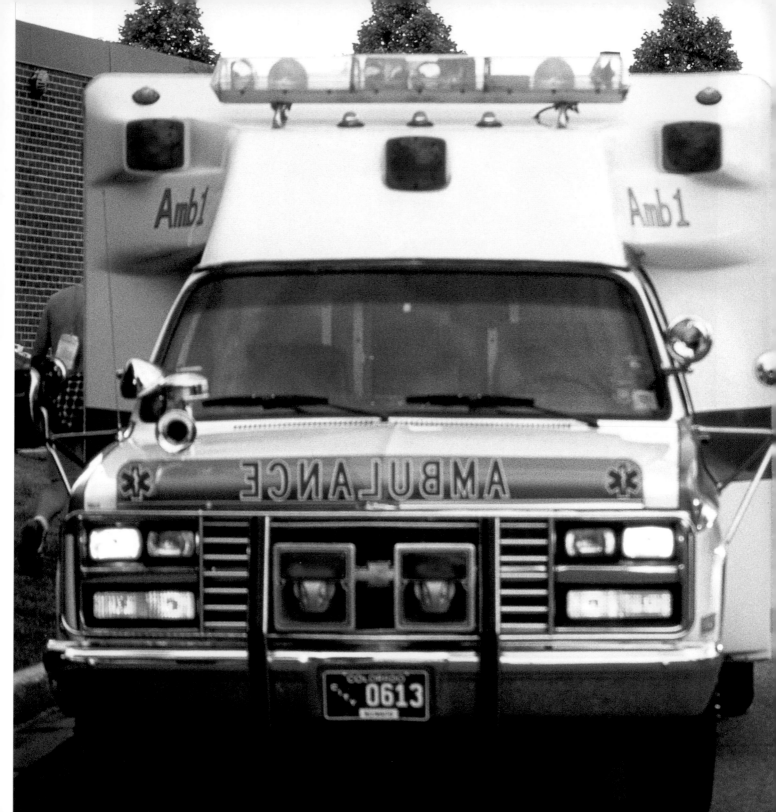

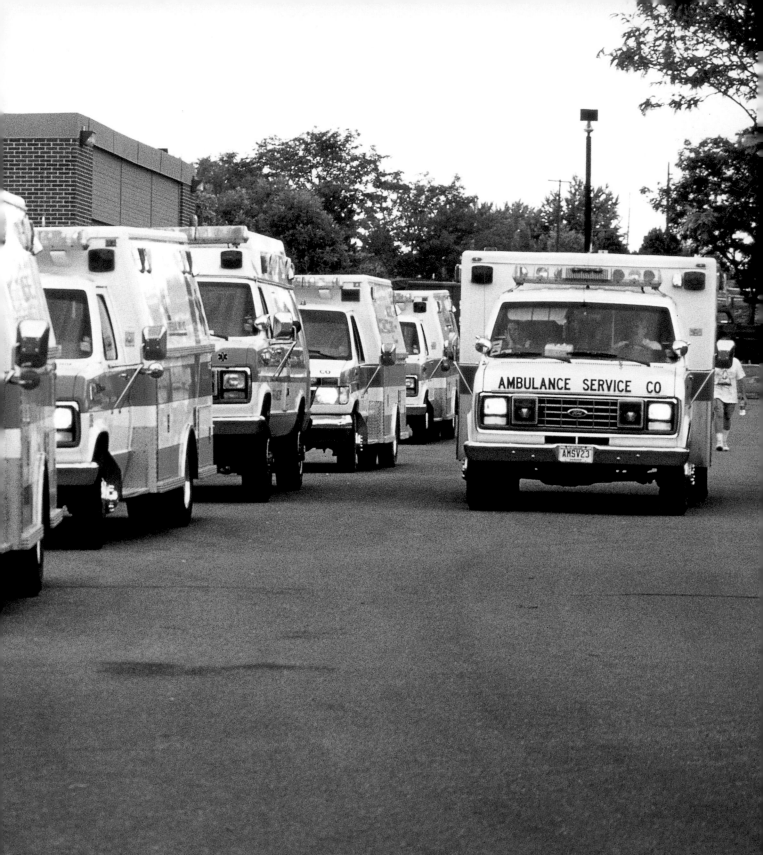

Most foreign countries do not share the luxuries found in large modular ambulances that are commonplace in the United States. This 1996 Chevrolet serves as a basic life support (BLS) unit for the fire department in Rio de Janeiro, Brazil. In most circumstances, BLS in foreign countries is more basic than in the United States, and advanced life support is rare. *Red Novecki*

down to the truck to sort out all of our equipment and prepare for the kids to arrive," Erickson explained. "Without the specialty training and equipment that we're given, we would never have been able to give those preemies the kind of respiratory support that they needed." Situations like these, and thousands more like them, prove the value of specialized, critical care transportation personnel and equipment, including the mobile intensive care units that "bring the big city hospital to the small town" every day.

The two babies survived the trip and were eventually removed from the ventilators and sent back to Waconia. The average 911 ambulance would have been able to get the twins back and forth just as quickly, but certainly would not have been equipped to deal with their serious conditions in the way that a highly advanced MICU can. The specialized training possessed by Lee Erickson and the NICU team is undoubtedly responsible for the effective, life-saving care that was provided to these tiny patients.

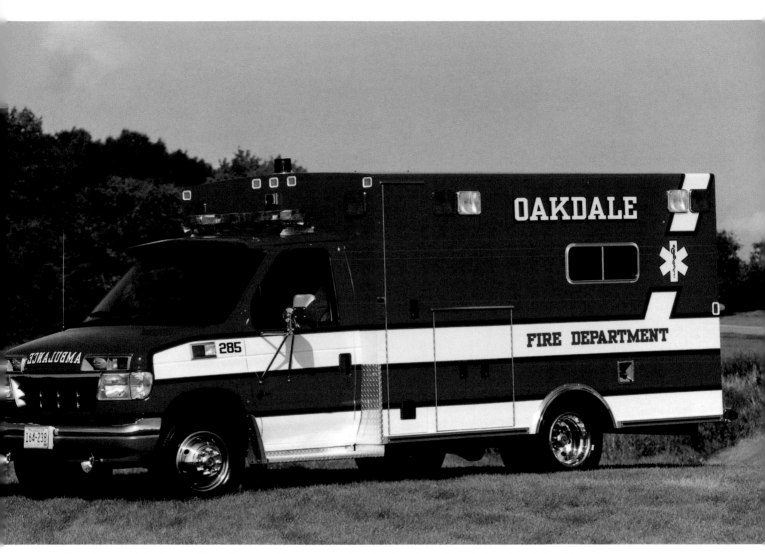

This sharp modular is one of Braun's successful attempts at deviating from its traditional slant-side design. Note the green strobe on the roof, used to establish command at a large scene. Also, the low-mounted air horns help keep the blast away from the crew. *Red Novecki*

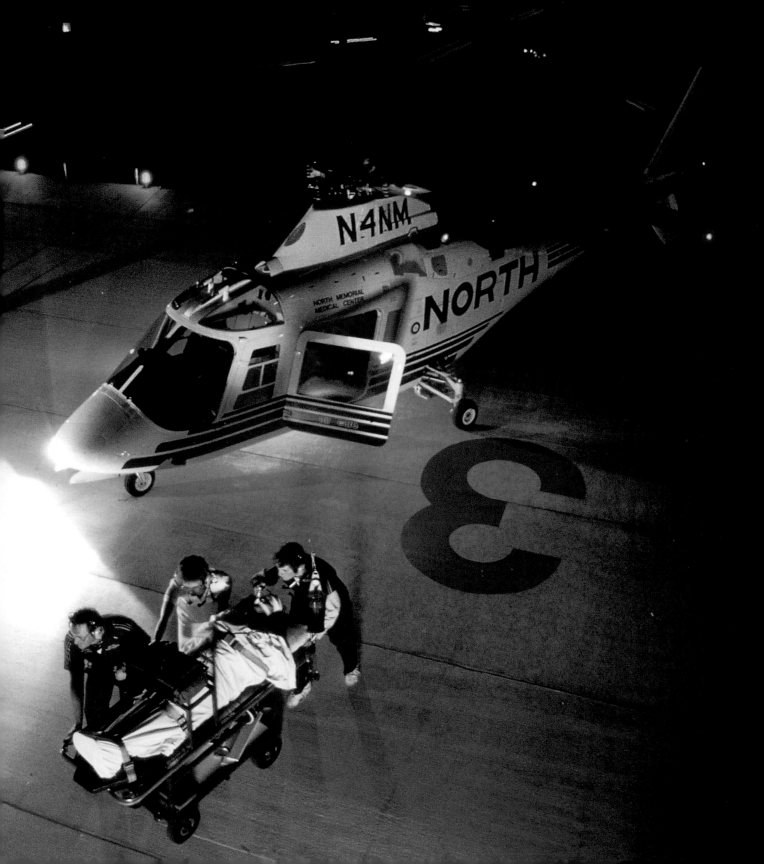

CHAPTER THREE

AIRCRAFT

Injured patients were first flown to safety more than 100 years ago, even before the first airplane or helicopter was invented. In 1870, approximately 160 wounded civilians and soldiers were evacuated by hot air balloon during the Prussian siege of Paris. Transporting patients by balloon, however, left the direction of travel up to the wind.

By the 1930s airplanes were being used to transport patients over long distances—a service they still provide. However, airplanes require runways that are not normally found at hospitals. Aerial transport of patients became more practical with the advent of the helicopter. Helicopters were first evaluated for this purpose during World War II. At that time, helicopter technology was still too immature for it to be of significant value. It was not until the Korean War in 1950, where U.S. Marine helicopters evacuated more than 10,000 casualties, that they began to demonstrate their worth. The Bell 47 landing with a pair of patients at the beginning of the 1970s TV series M*A*S*H* illustrates this bit of history well.

Rescue calls don't stop when the sun goes down. An Agusta A109 makes a late-night delivery of a critically ill patient. In flight, its retractable gear tucks away and enables the A109 to reach its maximum speed of 177 miles per hour. *Gary Bistram*

The power and size of helicopters increased considerably over the next 20 years. By the time fighting broke out in Vietnam, new helicopters like the Bell UH-1 "Huey" were ready for duty. The interior volume of these helicopters allowed the military to use them not only for evacuation, but to administer care to patients in flight. No longer did patients have to ride unattended on stretchers outside of the helicopter. During the Vietnam War, helicopters evacuated more than one million injured soldiers to safety.

During World War II, an average of 4.5 people died per 100 casualties that occurred. This figure dropped to 2.5 deaths per 100 in Korea, and to less than one death per 100 in Vietnam. Medical helicopters, along with other advancements, contributed greatly to this sharp decrease in the number of deaths during war. By the 1970s, the medical helicopter had finally come of age.

Back in the United States, the government realized the benefits of medical helicopters might be useful to the civilian population, too. When a study by the National Highway Safety Council showed the number of people killed in automobile accidents per year was higher than the number of soldiers killed during the Korean or Vietnam wars, Congress took notice. Congressional members remembered the value helicopters had shown during the wars and stated their support for them by pass-

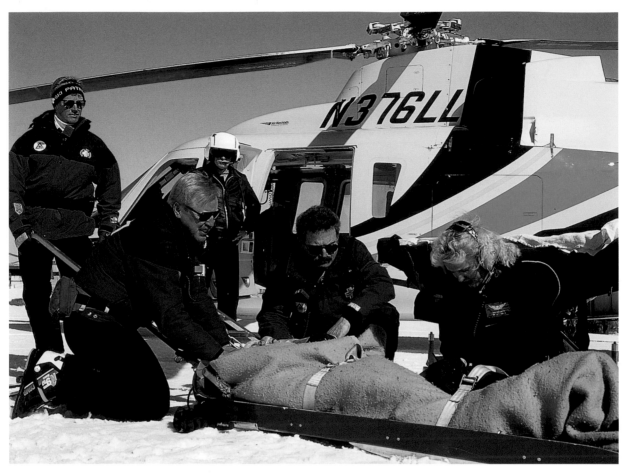

Given the right conditions, the S-76 is capable of landing right on a ski hill—a practice necessary for patients who should not be moved but need to get to the hospital. A patient with severe spinal problems can avoid the risk of further injury that may occur during a sled ride down the hill to an ambulance. *Life Link III*

ing the National Highway Safety Act, which said in part: "The helicopter is unsurpassed as a transportation tool in avoiding traffic congestion, speeding aid to the ill or injured in remote or inaccessible locations (which includes traffic jams), and rapidly transporting the injured to medical care centers . . . in the shortest practical time without simultaneously creating additional hazards."

The future role of the civilian medical helicopter was officially defined.

When distances are long and time is critical, there is no substitute for the speed of an aircraft. There are fixed-wing rescue aircraft capable of speeds up to 600 miles per hour, and their rotor-winged cousins are approaching 200 miles per hour. These speeds, coupled with the convenience of not needing roads and avoiding traffic, provide opportunities to save lives that otherwise would have been lost. Traveling "as the crow flies" enables an aircraft to cover approximately 1.2 ground miles for each straight air mile. When the aircraft's greater speed is factored in as well, the net effect is a transport time between one-third and one-fourth that required for the equivalent ground transportation.

Emergency rescue aircraft today are both highly sophisticated and expensive. With costs ranging from $500,000 to $10 million for a modern plane or helicopter, life-saving opportunities are costly to provide. At first, many municipalities found it hard to justify the high start-up and operating costs for a helicopter slated solely for use as an air ambulance. To justify the high costs, many cities, counties, and states made their helicopters "multipurpose" to spread the dollars out over many functions. A multipurpose helicopter is used for medical purposes, but also is used for police, fire, or government flights, too. In 1969, the Maryland State Police Department was the first governmental body to try the multi-use concept by using its police helicopters for medical runs. The Illinois Department of Transportation followed two years later when it began making medical, search and rescue, and state business flights.

In 1972, the first hospital-based air medical service went into operation at St. Anthony Hospital in Denver, Colorado. Known as Flight for Life, this program became a prototype for the entire industry. Air medical services began popping up around the United States slowly at first, with only a few new programs beginning each year. It wasn't until 1978 that the industry started to experience major growth, which has continued through today. Now there are hundreds of air medical

An AS 365N2 Dauphin from the Maryland State Police Department lowers a rescue basket called a Billy Pugh net. They were among the first to offer EMS helicopter service and now operate a system of eight helicopters with paramedics and rescue gear to cover the entire state. *Barry Smith*

A U.S. Coast Guard HH-60J lowers a rescue swimmer during a cliff-rescue training exercise on the California coast. The HH-60J, also known as the Jayhawk, is equipped with search and weather radar, sophisticated navigation electronics, and cockpit lighting to support the use of night-vision goggles for rescues after dark. *Barry Smith*

A fully equipped rescue swimmer wears an exposure suit to protect him from the cold, fins for swimming in high waves, a mask to keep the rotor wash out of his eyes, a personal flotation device, and a harness to latch the helicopter's hoist cable to. Once in the water a rescue swimmer can quickly calm a panicked victim and guide him or her to safety. *Barry Smith*

service programs in operation and more being implemented all over the world. Rescue aircraft have transported millions of patients in need.

Fixed- or rotor-wing, today's rescue aircraft, are usually specialized for one of two missions: those equipped for emergency medical service (EMS) and those equipped for search and rescue (SAR) operations. Since space and weight are limited, aircraft are normally outfitted for one role or the other, but not both. The type of rescue mission dictates which type of aircraft is best suited for the task. Although each carries some of the same basic medical equipment, their more advanced equipment is quite different.

Fixed-wing EMS aircraft transport patients over long distances, generally more than 150 miles. Interfacility transport, which involves transporting a patient from one hospital to another, is their most common role. A typical call might involve flying out to a small-town airport to pick up an organ-transplant patient on life support and delivering the patient to an airport near a hospital capable of performing the operation. Their combination of speed, highly trained crews, and advanced medical equipment makes these aircraft ideal for these missions. The aircraft are typically business jets or turboprops that have had their cabins modified, replacing their luxury seats with a stretcher surrounded by seats for the medics. Life-support equipment is installed to provide patients with their needs as they are moved from one hospital to another. Few hospitals have their own runways, so fixed-wing EMS aircraft usually require ambulance support on the ground at both their departure and arrival airports.

Fixed-wing SAR aircraft are operated primarily by the military and Coast Guard. These aircraft use sophisticated sensors to cover wide search areas to locate people in trouble. Their missions are primarily conducted out over the ocean, where long-range sensors can easily locate ships or aircraft in trouble. The U.S. Coast Guard flies the HU-25 Guardian in this role. These aircraft are

With rescue trucks in the background, a Bell 47 is about to take off to lift out an injured climber near Ouray, Colorado. The world's first mass-produced helicopter, the Bell 47 remains in strong demand due to its simplicity, reliability, and low cost. If the money is available, however, most rescue departments prefer a larger aircraft that can carry a stretcher internally. *Barry Smith*

quite ordinary looking on the outside, sharing the same structure as their business-jet cousin, the Dassault Falcon 200. But on the inside they are equipped with an APG-66 radar (which is also used on the F-16 fighter) and a Forward Looking Infra Red (FLIR) system. These systems allow the Guardian to locate and track sea and air traffic at great range, day or night, even in bad weather. Since few fixed-wing SAR aircraft are amphibious, they are limited to only locating people needing rescue, leaving the actual pickup work to helicopters and ships that they vector to the area.

Rotor-wing aircraft, more commonly known as helicopters, have the unique ability of being able to take off and land almost anywhere, making them well suited to rescue work. This utility comes at a cost, however. Helicopters are limited in range when compared to a fixed-wing aircraft. Most helicopters would be stretching their fuel limit making a round-trip flight to a hospital 150 miles away. If distances are greater than this, multiple fuel stops would be necessary to make the flight. Fuel stops can lengthen a helicopter's response time to a point where fixed-wing aircraft are faster, even though they cannot go directly to the hospital.

Fortunately, few places are more than 150 miles away from a hospital, so a few helicopters can easily provide coverage for a large area. EMS helicopters pro-

Perched on a rock in some of the rugged and inaccessible terrain within the city, a Bell 412 of the Los Angeles City Fire Department drops off supplies for a nearby fire crew. The fire department uses this helicopter to drop water on fires, respond to medical emergencies, and rescue people with its hoist. *Barry Smith*

vide three types of service to their surrounding communities: interfacility transport (the most common), followed by direct pick-up or scene response, and finally the transport of medical personnel and supplies. These three roles, as you will read, each presents its own challenges to an EMS helicopter crew.

Helicopter interfacility transports involve the transfer of patients from hospital to hospital. For example, a patient in a rural hospital having multiple-trauma injuries would need to be moved to a tertiary-care facility or regional trauma center. Or perhaps a physician feels that the additional care and special equipment found only in a larger hospital is required.

Interfacility transports are used when a patient, such as a premature infant, requires a specific specialty-care unit to keep them healthy. In each of these cases, a helicopter would fly out and pick up the patient at the local hospital and deliver the patient to one more suited to his or her needs.

Direct helicopter pickup of patients falls into two categories, first or secondary responder. A helicopter acting as a first responder is necessary in situations where patients are either in an inaccessible location for ground EMS or where they would have to wait too long for it to arrive. Situations such as traffic jams or emergencies in off-road or remote locations can make a helicopter the fastest

Noisy, cramped, and jostled by turbulence, the cabin of a helicopter is not the ideal place for critically ill patients. Even so, the experience and equipment of a helicopter crew often allows them to provide a level of care not possible in many rural hospitals. *Gary Bistram*

alternative in an emergency. As a secondary responder, a helicopter responds to an accident scene after other care providers have arrived. This is often the case with bad car accidents where passengers must be extricated from a mangled vehicle. Ground EMS normally arrives on the scene first, followed by a rescue truck with extrication tools. They begin caring for patients in the vehicle while working to free them from it. During this time, a helicopter can be en route, enabling it to be on the scene when the patient finally is freed. The helicopter can then take the injured person directly to the hospital.

When transporting medical teams and supplies, a helicopter would normally pick up a team and its gear

at a base hospital and fly to the patient at an outlying facility or emergency scene. This allows expert physicians, transplant organs, blood products, or certain medications to be available anywhere within the helicopter's range. This can be critical to a patient whose health depends on not being moved.

SAR helicopters, like their fixed-wing cousins, are operated primarily by the military, and most notably the U.S. Coast Guard. These helicopters are designed for the same roles as fixed-wing SAR aircraft, but obviously have the ability to hover and pick up people. A typical distress call for a coastal SAR helicopter might involve picking up an injured crew member off a fishing

The Cessna 441 Conquest is a pressurized, twin-engined turboprop that can cruise at altitudes up to 30,000 feet, enabling it to ride comfortably above most turbulent weather on flights ranging over 1,000 nautical miles. *Life Link III*

trawler working offshore. In the past, the only way to find such a vessel was to rely on primitive navigation systems or even dead reckoning, neither of which are very accurate. These procedures only get the helicopter into the general area, and then its pilot must search

many square miles of ocean and make sure the right ship is found among any in the area. Today's ships often call in emergencies on cellular telephones, and Global Positioning System (GPS) navigation equipment is almost universal. Both of these devices are frequently

While the medics take care of patients in back, the pilot monitors the instrument panel of the helicopter up front. On the rare occasion something goes seriously wrong up here, the patient and crew can be in great danger. Unlike airplanes, helicopters do not glide well. *Gary Bistram*

carried onboard even the smallest boats. Still, GPS has not been fully certified for use in aerial navigation. Therefore, a helicopter can only use it to cross-check and verify traditional radio beacons and distance-measuring equipment on the way to a scene. GPS can be used only once the helicopter has arrived near the scene and switched from instrument to visual navigation.

A helicopter headed out to a trawler in an offshore area would cruise to the area at 5,000 feet, which optimizes engine efficiency and radio performance. The high altitude allows VHF communications with the base to extend to approximately 100 miles. In an ideal

case, a fixed-wing SAR aircraft will go out and do the initial search for the vessel and update its position for the helicopter. This information can be crucial; a helicopter can only go out a maximum of approximately 150 miles and still have enough fuel to return. The helicopter can obviously spend more time hovering or "loi-

After arriving quickly on-scene to this farm accident, this Bell 222 is standing by to transport. Like many light-utility helicopters, the 222 carries its patients lengthwise, with their legs extending into the cockpit area beside the pilot. Space is a premium aboard any rescue helicopter. *Peter Beck*

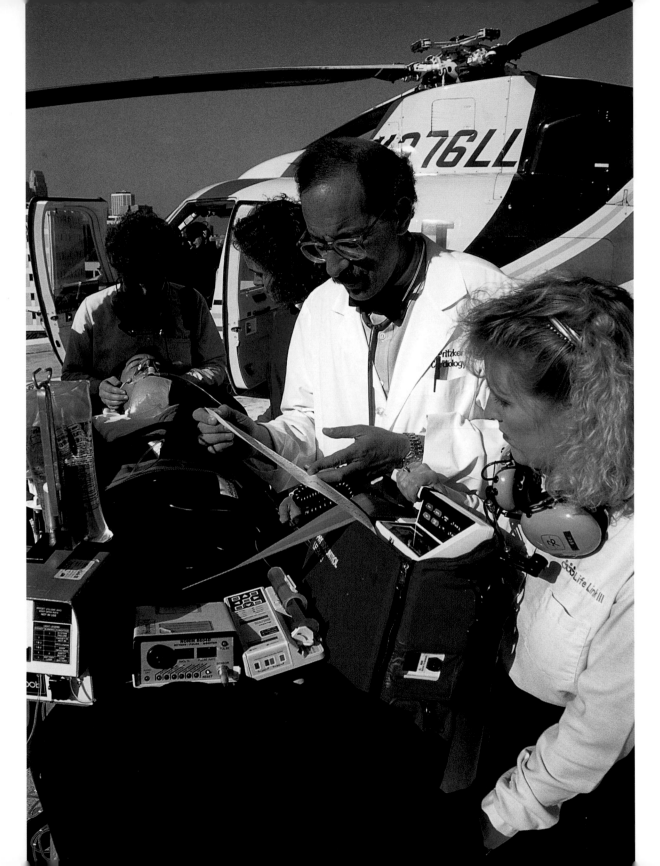

A medic's-eye view from the helicopter on touchdown at the scene of a motorcycle accident. Equipped with portable medical equipment relevant to the injuries described on the radio, the medics must spring into action as soon as the helicopter touches down, making every second count. *North Memorial Medical Center*

tering" on scene as the distance between the base and the helicopter gets closer.

Because of a helicopter's limited fuel supply, search time is critical. To land a medic/crew member, stabilize the casualty, and recover both the patient and medic can take up to 20 minutes. Since a helicopter uses less fuel at cruising speeds than it does in a hover, the pilot

On the hospital helipad, a cardiologist examines the EKG readout on a new arrival. The portable equipment on the stretcher includes (left to right) an IV pump, a pulse oxymeter, a syringe pump, and a Lifepak 10 portable defibrillator. *Life Link III*

will calculate a descent from 5,000 feet down into the search area. A fuel-efficient, high-airspeed, gradual descent may add the critical margin of fuel required to save a life. Once the helicopter is below 500 feet, the autopilot is activated by selecting an approach profile. This engages the radar altimeter, allowing the helicopter to maintain speed and follow the descent profile down to 200 feet. Once at 200 feet, the pilot can slow to around 90 knots and search for the vessel visually, using the autopilot to maintain altitude.

When the vessel is located, the pilot undertakes a "mark on target" profile to position the helicopter over it for the rescue. First the pilot flies over the ves-

✚ The Flying Hospital

Ever see a hospital capable of more than 450 knots and a range of more than 3,000 nautical miles? This Lockheed L-1011 TriStar airliner was modified into a fully functional flying hospital capable of surgery, emergency medical treatment, and dental care. Operation Blessing International Relief and Development Corporation aims to use this aircraft to deliver medical care to needy people in remote, impoverished places. Since it is designed to operate without any support facilities, it is completely self-sustaining. It can operate on its own power for up to 10 hours per day for 10 consecutive days. Once it has arrived at its destination, the L-1011 unloads its auxiliary power unit and diesel generator so the crew can place them next to the aircraft to provide power during working hours. When all the systems are powered and on-line, the aircraft is ready to treat patients.

At 164 feet long, the L-1011 has ample room for many of the amenities of a hospital. A patient would enter the aircraft on the lower deck and be processed in the patient check-in/check-out room. From there they would be sent to the area corresponding to their ills: the main operating room that can simultaneously handle three separate surgeries; a two-chair dental area that doubles as an ear-nose-and-throat treatment facility; two trauma/triage rooms for treating medical emergencies; the pharmacy for medicine dispensing; or the multipurpose area that serves as a 12-bed pre- and postoperative suite.

It carries its own sterilization and waste disposal capabilities. It also has a supply of medical gases (carbon dioxide, nitrous oxide, partial vacuum for suction, and pressurized air). This includes its own oxygen-generation system that can convert outside air into medical-quality oxygen. A self-contained environmental control system provides the aircraft with an environment suitable for an operating room. It even has its own water purification system, a 150-gallon water-storage tank, and food storage onboard.

As this is the first "flying hospital," many companies are anxious to study the business aspects of operating the aircraft. Those directly involved in funding it can already see other potential opportunities for airborne medical facilities. Perhaps someday flying hospitals will be used by multinational businesses with remote field operations to bring care to employees. The U.S. military currently operates the C-9 Nightingale (a converted DC-9) for emergency medicine. Perhaps someday it will see a need for flying hospitals to supplement the Nightingale. At only $25 million for a fully converted L-1011, flying hospitals could easily be cheaper than building and staffing conventional hospitals in certain areas. If nothing else, they at least proved it can be done.

George Hall/Check Six

This Agusta A109 Max is operated jointly by North Memorial Medical Center and the Hennepin County Medical Center in Minneapolis, Minnesota. A U.S. firm engineered the upward-opening side doors and fairings to give the Italian-made helicopter a larger and more-accessible cabin, thus adding the "Max" designation to an ordinary A109. *Jeffrey Grosscup*

sel and registers its position in the NAV system with the push of a button. The helicopter then enters a downwind circuit, automatically ending up in a 40-foot hover, 150 feet behind the vessel on its port side. The pilot can then inch the helicopter up to a position directly over the boat, where the winchman will signal to hold the position. The autopilot can compensate for the wind while the pilot maintains overall authority. The winchman lowers a medic/crew member and gear down onto the deck, where the medic releases the harness when his or her feet hit the boat. Once the medic/crew member on deck is clear, the

Although originally developed to transport business executives, the Learjet 24D turned out to be an excellent aircraft for long-distance medical transfers. Capable of cruising 1,300 miles at over 400 knots at altitudes up to 51,000 feet, Learjets can fly most places at high speed, nonstop, and above inclement weather, thus minimizing a patient's time between hospitals. *Learjet, Inc.*

The Russian Mi-26 is indisputably the largest helicopter in the world. At over 26 feet from the ground to the top of the rotor head, it is taller than a two-story building. The medical version, known as the Mi-26MS, carries a flight crew of 4, a medical team of 9, and up to 15 patients in sections designated for increasing care levels: ambulatory, life support, pre-op, and surgery. This one is resting between flights at a Russian air force base. *Mark Wagner*

Two members of the National Ski Patrol stand by as Life Link III's Sikorsky S-76 prepares to land. While most helicopters can trace their roots back to an original military design, the S-76 was designed from the ground up for commercial use. *Life Link III*

With its extendable refueling probe reaching clear of the rotors, this Sikorsky HH-60G is maneuvering into position for air-to-air refueling from a C-130 tanker. The HH-60G is a combat rescue helicopter used to retrieve U.S. military pilots downed deep behind enemy lines. They also perform many civil rescue missions each year from bases around the United States. *Barry Smith*

Whether fixed- or rotor-wing, EMS or SAR, rescue aircraft and their crews provide live-saving service to thousands of people every year. They can cover hundreds of square miles, providing advanced medical care and swift access to hospitals for patients who cannot wait for conventional ground transportation or are in areas where it will never come. If ground transportation time for a rescue run is predicted to be less than 20 minutes, it is usually best to transport that patient by ground. But if distances or obstacles make ground transport longer than that, a rescue aircraft can usually arrive faster, making it the obvious choice in an emergency.

Members of the Capitol City Fire and Rescue Department of Juneau, Alaska, treat a near-drowning victim next to a glacier-fed lake. The department uses a Eurocopter AS 350 Ecureuil (Squirrel) provided by a local helicopter tour company for use during emergencies. *Barry Smith*

A U.S. Coast Guard HH-65A Dolphin retrieves a rescue swimmer on a training mission. The HH-65A has twin Textron Lycoming LTS 101 powerplants that together develop more than 1,300 horsepower, allowing it to hover with considerable power in reserve. The Coast Guard operates nearly 100 of these helicopters. *Barry Smith*

CHAPTER FOUR

WATER RESCUE

For people in search of the ultimate vacation spot, a body of water is often an essential ingredient. Be it a swimming pool, lake, river, or ocean, people tend to gravitate toward the water's edge for a multitude of reasons. Swimming, fishing, surfing, and boating are on most everyone's minds whenever the sun is shining. Millions of people flock to the water every year for recreation. There are also those who make their livings out on the waves. Commercial fishers, offshore oil rig workers, marine biologists, and merchant mariners are just a few who spend a good portion of their lives on the water. These people leave the relative safety of dry land every day, whether the sun is shining or not.

Whether for work or play, the shear volume of people interacting with various bodies of water makes it inevitable that some will get into trouble and need help getting out of it. Rescue crews stand by around the world for such emergencies, waiting for a cry for help. These crews man a wide variety of rescue craft, each specialized for its particular mission. Ranging from high-tech, sea-going hovercraft, down to small flat-bottom boats with outboard motors, they all are made to facilitate the rescue of people in danger.

Water presents a time-consuming obstacle between any patient and rescue. During water rescues, vehicles are often invaluable for performing a rescue within the golden hour (the first hour after an accident, the most critical time for survival). Often a simple boat is the perfect answer to reach a patient, but sometimes circumstances make boats more trouble than they're worth. For example, many airports have water or wetland areas around their runways to allow aircraft to come and go in places where noise will not be an issue with homeowners. In the event of a plane crash in one of these areas, the marshes are wet enough to prevent a standard ambulance from responding. At the same time, they are not deep enough for even a small boat to operate.

Now that the Federal Aviation Administration and other aviation authorities are paying more attention to the details of responding to an airplane crash in these areas, airport rescue teams are using the abilities of a new member of the rescue vehicle field: hovercraft. Since they ride on a cushion of air trapped underneath them by a rubber skirt system,

A U.S. Coast Guard 30-foot Surf-Rescue boat powers into an oncoming wave. With their self-bailing, self-righting design, these boats are specifically built to operate in heavy seas. Each crew member is secured by a safety harness to make sure they stay aboard when the waves crash over the deck. *Barry Smith*

The Canadian Coast Guard uses this rescue hovercraft off the coast of British Columbia. Hovercraft are particularly useful for operations in shallow water, thin ice, and low-lying areas where they can transition directly from operating over the water to dry ground. *Barry Smith*

hovercraft can travel over land, water, ice, snow, mud, or marsh with relative ease. Thus, they can go places where boats, jet-skis, inflatables, all-terrain vehicles, and snowmobiles cannot. A hovercraft could respond directly from an airport rescue station, traveling down a taxiway to the end of the runway and move out into a marsh without even slowing down. On the way to a crash site, it could easily traverse small islands, beds of reeds, or patches of deep open water. The ability to cross such a wide variety of terrain is what allows them

to reach certain areas more quickly than anything else. Once on the scene, the crew could deploy inflatable rafts for the survivors and begin to evacuate the most critically injured.

Departments are also finding them useful for swift-water rescue. A fast-moving stream or river can be a challenge to any boat, which would have to use its engine power to fight the current at all times to hold position. A hovercraft's hull does not ride in the water, so it does not have to fight the current. No matter how fast the water is moving, it just flows

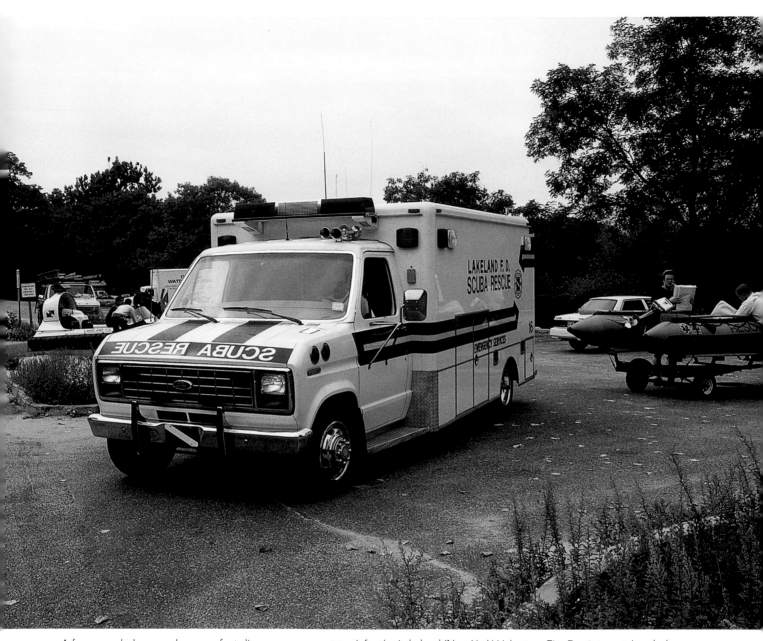

A former ambulance makes a perfect dive rescue support truck for the Lakeland (New York) Volunteer Fire Department. Loaded with scuba tanks, regulators, wet suits, dive computers, masks, fins, and snorkels, it carries equipment that is impractical to keep on an ordinary ambulance. *Barry Smith*

✚ The World's Largest Rescue Vehicles

It's probably no surprise that the world's largest rescue vehicles are owned by the U.S. Department of Defense. The Pentagon converted two San-Clemente class tankers into the hospital ships USNS Mercy and USNS Comfort in 1986 and 1987. Nearly three football fields long, the hospital ships provide emergency, on-site combat surgical, and medical care to U.S. military forces during wartime and contingencies.

The two hospital ships are part of the Military Sealift Command's Strategic Sealift Force. Each ship contains 1,000 hospital beds, 12 operating rooms, radiological services, medical laboratories, an optometry lab, a pharmacy, and two oxygen-producing plants. These ships are larger than any shore-based naval medical facility and each has a helicopter deck large enough to receive injured personnel from even the largest military helicopters.

USNS Comfort. U.S. Navy

Ordinarily, the ships are kept in reduced operating status and maintained by a small crew of civilian mariners and a cadre of Navy medical and communications specialists. They can be activated, fully staffed, and ready to get under way in only five days. When activated, each has more than 800 active-duty Navy personnel from the Navy's medical organization, 380 Navy support and communications personnel, and 62 U.S. Civil Service mariners to operate the ship.

To keep the ships ready to deploy anywhere in the world, they are kept on separate coasts of the United States: the USNS *Mercy* on the West Coast in Oakland, California, and USNS *Comfort* on the East Coast in Baltimore, Maryland. The nearest ship to a crisis is usually sent if the crisis is small enough to be handled by one ship. Both ships were activated and sent to the Middle East to provide medical support for Operation Desert Storm. Fortunately, little of their capacity was needed.

With a five-day prep time and a top speed of less than 18 knots, these ships are not exactly fast at getting anywhere. Once they arrive, they add an entire hospital to an area in need. If no large port facilities are available at their destination, they can anchor offshore and use helicopters and launches as shuttles to and from the ship to service more remote areas.

Conversion: National Steel and Shipbuilding Company, San Diego, California
Powerplant: geared steam turbine, two boilers, one shaft, 24,500 shaft horsepower
Length: 894 feet
Beam: 106 feet
Displacement: 69,360 tons (full load)
Speed: 17.5 knots (20 miles per hour)

USNS Mercy. U.S. Navy

This small hovercraft enables the Lakeland Volunteer Fire Department to quickly get into areas inaccessible to large boats. Although not an ideal vehicle for patient transport, it is useful to either deliver a medic to a scene or to get a victim out of immediate danger. *Barry Smith*

underneath. A standard boat that finds itself sideways in a fast current is swept quickly downstream, while a hovercraft maintains its course and maneuvers as commanded. Hovercraft are useful for searching up narrow creeks and rivers where water depth and current may inhibit the use of conventional craft.

People who fall through the ice on a frozen lake would definitely appreciate a nearby hovercraft. To the hovercraft, there is no difference between thin ice and open water. Both are flat surfaces that the air

cushion can ride on. To rescue someone, all the crew must do is drive out directly to them and pick them up. It does not matter if the ice can support the weight or not. The result is a fast, efficient rescue that otherwise would have required sliding a small boat on the ice by hand—a time-consuming process that the victim cannot always wait for.

In tidal flats, the receding tide can often leave unsuspecting boaters stranded in the shallows or deep in mud. Hovercraft quickly traverse these

With its 375-horsepower diesel engine, a U.S. Coast Guard Surf-Rescue boat can speed along at 28 knots in calm water. But in seas like this, the throttle must be carefully managed for the boat to maintain its course and keep its bow pointed into the waves. *Barry Smith*

NEXT: For use in nearby lakes, the Truckee (California) Fire Department values the shallow water abilities of this air boat in summer and its over-ice capabilities in winter. Here the crew is launching the craft onto a frozen lake. *Barry Smith*

Once out on the ice, the Truckee air boat can reach speeds up to 70 miles per hour if necessary. Due to a lack of brakes, maneuvers like this must be carefully executed. *Barry Smith*

This rescue boat belongs to the Capitol City Fire and Rescue Department in Juneau, Alaska. Flat-bottom boats like these are ideal rescue platforms on smaller waters due to their wide, stable design. *Barry Smith*

areas just as easily as they would open water and can provide assistance immediately instead of waiting for the tide to come back in. In the event of a flood, hovercraft are ideal for moving in and around deeply flooded neighborhoods. Floodwaters are always murky, and it is difficult to tell what may be just below the surface as you travel along. Submerged objects such as automobiles, mailboxes, and fences can quickly stop an outboard motor. Hovercraft need only worry about the objects above the surface, which are clearly visible in daylight hours. When they are equipped with searchlights, they work at night, too.

All of these special circumstances make hovercraft uniquely capable vehicles that can be great assets to rescue teams in a variety of situations. Even

LEFT: The San Francisco Fire Department rides Yamaha personal watercraft for quick-response rescues in the surf. Although originally designed as pleasure craft, the SFFD found them great for quickly reaching swimmers in trouble. *Barry Smith*

BELOW: The National Park Service uses its inflatable boats to reach swimmers and surfers in trouble in the San Francisco area. Both lightweight and stable, inflatable boats are ideal for getting around quickly in the surf. *Barry Smith*

Although based on an older Ford chassis, this four-wheel-drive truck operated by the San Francisco Fire Department is perfectly suited to move its crew and equipment up and down the beach. A pair of sea kayaks can be easily deployed after the truck arrives on scene. *Barry Smith*

though the military and parts of the civilian world have used hovercraft for years, they are just beginning to be embraced by the rescue community. Their value is being recognized by many rescue departments that seek an effective, versatile watercraft for rescue operations.

Whether they use hovercraft, airboats, rubber rafts, or cabin cruisers, water rescue teams rely on a wide variety of craft that are specially suited for the roles most likely needed by their communities.

Departments must constantly be ready for water rescues in their area. They also must be prepared to assist at any nearby special events in or around the water. Rescue crews often stand by at

these events waiting for accidents to happen, especially in the case of dangerous sports such as racing.

A Hydroplane Racing Rescue

It was the Grand National Hydroplane Boat Races in Essex, Maryland. Just like at every event in this race series, an emergency medical crew was on hand. Two rescue boats and their respective crews floated in the center of the race course, while an

This U.S. Coast Guard rigid-hull inflatable boat (RIB) is well suited for all types of rescue work. With its combination fiberglass/inflatable hull, it is stable at high speeds and can still carry a large load. This model is built by Zodiac. *Barry Smith*

The U.S. Coast Guard's 47-foot motor lifeboats were built with a stable, deep-V hull form. These aluminum-hulled boats were first launched in 1990 to replace the older, slower 44-footers. Its twin diesels generate 850 horsepower, enabling them to make 25 knots—nearly twice as fast as the old ones. *Barry Smith*

ambulance stood by on shore among the fans. In the event of a crash, the rescue boat and ambulance work in combination to transport an injured driver quickly to the hospital.

The Carolina Skiffs—small, flat-bottomed boats used by the rescue teams working for the American Powerboat Racing Association—never need to go far for a rescue, as they are always standing by on the course during boat races. They do, however, need to get their crews and equipment to the scene quickly.

On any given day of racing, hydroplanes speed side by side, easily reaching 150 miles per hour on the straightaway as they attempt to gain a favorable line for the next turn. Though safety is a primary concern of everyone involved, several thousand pounds of boats, incredible speeds, and aggressive drivers make the odds of maintaining perfect safety difficult. For hydroplane No. 7, also known as *Hot Ticket*, this day was going to be more difficult than normal.

Hot Ticket's driver, Patrick O'Conner, was pushing it as he tried to make up for a bad start. Through his windshield he could see the other boats he had to catch. Both hands firmly on the wheel, he pushed hard on the accelerator pedal for more speed. His hydroplane packed an alcohol-fueled Chevrolet big block. The acceleration generated by the highly tuned engine pushed him firmly back in his seat. He was on the main straight as his boat approached 160 miles per hour.

Cursing himself for falling behind and getting "hosed down" by the rooster tail of a boat in front of him, he had to push hard to get back in the race. He burned down the main straight throwing a stream of

To rescue vessels adrift near dangerous reefs or rocks, the 47-foot motor lifeboat has the ability to tow craft up to 150 tons displacement. Even though when fully loaded it weighs nearly 18 tons itself, here it is seen nearly clear out of the water in heavy swells. *Barry Smith*

water high behind him. Patrick knew he was running out of time; the lead boat had only one lap to go.

Unfortunately, a small crosswind on the course that day had put a light chop on the water. As the boat powered down the straight, it skipped across the wave tops and air streamed beneath the hull. A poorly timed gust of wind was all it took to lift the nose a little too far, beginning an incredible chain reaction. Patrick felt the nose of the boat come up; instinctively he eased back on the throttle in an attempt to bring it down, but it was too late. The nose had lifted just enough to make the entire boat act as an airfoil, and like any wing, it was ready to fly.

The weight of the boat was nothing compared to the lift generated by the 160-mile-per-hour slipstream. The boat leapt off the water and hurdled 40 feet in the air. From inside the driver's safety capsule, the normal view of the horizon disappeared. All Patrick could see was sky. The boat was still moving quite fast when it came back down, hit the water, and flipped over many times. Surrounded by clouds of flying water, the boat cartwheeled off the end of the race course into shallow water. It finally landed upside down with a splash stained dark with mud.

Immediately the rescue teams went into action. As the rescue boats responded, the race referee put out the red flag. This signaled all the other boats to pull their kill switches and stop, so the rescue boats would not have to worry about navigating through 150-mile-per-hour traffic to reach the crash site. Each of the two rescue boats had a crew of five: a driver, two certified rescue divers, a "swimmer," and a paramedic. The driver's jobs are to drive the boat and coordinate the rescue; the rescue divers are available for underwater work; the swimmer's job is to help get the injured person out of the water and into the boat; and the paramedic cares for them once they are onboard. The crews of both boats were under the command of the

medical safety rescue director for the event, Brian Small. He was responsible for driving one of the boats and coordinating the entire team on scene. Aside from their highly trained crews, each boat carried a basic trauma kit, a supply of airway management equipment, a V-Vac (a hand-powered portable suction device), cervical collars specially sized for use with the race driver's helmets, and a rescue basket to maneuver patients in and out of the boat easily.

Brian's rescue boat arrived at the overturned boat first, and two rescue divers decked out in full scuba gear immediately jumped overboard before the boat had even come to a complete stop. They quickly swam over to the overturned race boat and submerged. They soon discovered that the boat was sitting in very shallow water and the canopy was buried in the muddy bottom, making it impossible to open from underneath. The driver was trapped inside and the extent of his injuries from the crash were unknown. The other rescue boat arrived, and one of its divers climbed on top of the overturned boat. The only way to get the driver out without moving the overturned boat was through the escape hatch. Each race boat has a 2-foot-square escape hatch in the bottom directly underneath the driver. Even so, it's not just a matter of opening the hatch and pulling the driver out. The cockpit of a racing hydroplane is similar in size to the cockpit of an Indy car in that there's room for the driver and little else. When a driver gets into a boat, he wiggles himself in and secures himself in a five-point safety harness. Then the removable steering wheel is attached and the canopy is closed, sealing him in.

Immediately after opening the hatch, it became apparent to the rescue crew that Patrick was unconscious. Time was of the essence. To get him out, they first had to remove the steering wheel—normally a simple matter when the boat is right side up. The rescue diver had to lay down on the bottom of the over-

A three-person crash-rescue crew stands by for the launch of an E-2C Hawkeye radar surveillance plane from the catapult of the aircraft carrier USS *Abraham Lincoln*. Since the flight deck on an aircraft carrier is more than 1,000 feet long, miniature fire-rescue trucks are needed to quickly move crews, equipment, and their patients around. *Barry Smith*

turned boat and reach into the hatch as far as he could just to get his hands on the wheel and then fumble with the attachment to get it off. Once the steering wheel was out of the way, the driver's five-point safety harness was next. Fortunately, the harnesses are equipped with a quick-release mechanism that enables them to be unbuckled easily, so it came off in a matter of seconds.

Even with everything out of the way, it was still not easy to extract the driver. All race drivers wear life jackets and helmets, making it difficult to fit them through the small escape hatches. With an unconscious driver unable to assist in any way, the difficulty is increased by a factor of ten. So after much pushing and pulling, bending and tugging, the driver finally was removed from the boat, feet first.

He was transferred immediately to a rescue boat floating alongside. The driver's helmet was removed, revealing that he had already started turning blue. He had no pulse and was not breathing. The rescue crew quickly went to work. One team member began chest compressions while another started breathing for him with an Ambu Bag. The rescue crew worked methodically and professionally, not wasting a moment of time. While the team was working the patient, Brian got the rescue boat headed into shore and was on the radio signaling

the ambulance to meet them at the dock, ready to transport. Fortunately, rescue radios were tuned to their own separate frequency from that of the race committee. This kept emergency communications on a clear, chatter-free channel. The ambulance received the request and acknowledged it.

By the time the rescue boat reached the dock, the medical team's efforts had restored consciousness to the driver. He was transferred promptly to the ambulance and brought to the hospital. After a thorough checkup it was determined that Patrick would be fine after a little rest. The rescue crew had saved his life. If the rescue boats had not been standing by during this race, any rescue attempts originating from shore would have taken far too long to get to the overturned boat. For a rescue boat or a racing boat, having the right equipment and highly trained personnel to run it are essential for success. Patrick and Brian both raced boats again, although for entirely different reasons. Patrick later raced again for the checkered flag, while Brian raced to the next accident.

Every day water rescue crews and their vehicles come to the aid of troubled people trapped in waters around the world. Thanks to the dedicated efforts of the crew, most of these people are not in trouble for long.

INDEX